MEN-AT-ARMS SERIES

EDITOR: MARTIN WINDROW

Grenada 1983

Text *by* LEE E. RUSSELL
and M. ALBERT MENDEZ

Colour plates by PAUL HANNON

OSPREY PUBLISHING LONDON

Published in 1985 by
Osprey Publishing Ltd
Member company of the George Philip Group
12–14 Long Acre, London WC2E 9LP
© Copyright 1985 Osprey Publishing Ltd
Reprinted 1985 (twice), 1986

British Library Cataloguing in Publication Data

Russell, Lee E.
    Grenada 1983.—(Men-at-Arms series, 159)
    1. Grenada—History, Military
    I. Title   II. Series
    972.98'45   F2056

ISBN 0-85045-583-9

Filmset in Great Britain
Printed in Hong Kong

Acknowledgements
The authors wish to express their appreciation to the
following organisations and individuals for their help
in researching this book:
    The Public Affairs Offices of the US Army, Navy,
Air Force and Marine Corps in New York City; the
Center for Military History, and the Public Affairs
Offices of the US State Department, Department of
Defense and Department of the Army, Washington
DC; the Public Affairs Offices of the following units or
commands: (Army) FORCECOM, XVIII ABN
CORPS, 82nd ABN DIV, 101st ABN DIV (AIR
ASLT) and 2/75th RANGER BN; (Marine Corps)
2nd MAR DIV and Camp Lejeune; (Navy)
ATLANTIC FLEET HQ; (Air Force) MILITARY
AIRLIFT COMMAND. All of these provided
photographs or information, and their personnel
cheerfully answered questions and obtained details of
operations and equipment.
    While it is unfair to single out individuals, the
authors wish to thank especially Mr Steven Strumvall
(FORCECOM) and Maj. Barry Wiley (82nd) for
their help. We also wish to thank the Defence Forces
of Barbados and Jamaica, and their consular offices in
New York; Mr Scott Minerbrook of Long Island
Newsday; Mr Kevin Steele of *Soldier of Fortune*
magazine; Mr Severino Mendez, Mr Fred Depkin,
SGM EFK, Mr Andreas Constantinou, Mr André
LaSalle and the students of the St George's University
Medical School, Grenada. Nevertheless, all opinions,
conclusions and inferences are those of the authors.

The 'New Jewel' Movement

The island of Grenada was first discovered by Columbus in 1498 on his third voyage to the New World. Thereafter, it passed through Spanish and French hands, and finally came under British ownership during the 18th century. Nutmeg and spices were introduced during the reign of George III, and soon became the island's chief export, remaining so until the present day. England governed Grenada directly as part of its Windward Islands Administration until the late 1950s. Early in the next decade, Britain sponsored two attempts to form her Caribbean colonies into a single federation. Failing in this, the individual islands were given independence within the British Commonwealth system, starting with Grenada in 1974. The island's first Prime Minister was the eccentric Sir Eric Gairy, a former trade union organiser. Gairy's administration combined a bizarre foreign policy with corruption and political repression at home. In March 1979 he was overthrown in a bloodless coup led by Maurice Bishop, a political rival long respected for his opposition to Gairy and his henchmen.

Bishop took power as head of Grenada's Provisional Revolutionary Government (PRG) in the name of his NEW JEWEL Movement Party: an acronym that stood for Joint Endeavor for Welfare, Education and Liberation. As in many Third World countries, the new leadership faced both political and economic problems, and Bishop and the NJM saw a solution in the example of Communist Cuba. Over the next four years they invited increasing assistance from both Cuba and other Communist states. This, plus Bishop's disinterest in holding elections, brought the PRG into conflict with American foreign policy in the region. The situation was aggravated by the PRG's announcement of its most ambitious project, a new international airport at Point Salines at the south of the island.

To be built largely by Cuban workers, it featured a 9,000 ft runway—enough to take the largest jet aircraft. Its ostensible purpose was to improve Grenada's sagging tourist trade (the existing Pearls Airport could accept only twin-engined air traffic), but documents captured later also indicate a military potential. The Cubans planned to use the airport as a staging base for airlifting supplies to their troops in Africa, and as a refuelling stop for Soviet planes en route to Nicaragua. Work began in late 1979, and was scheduled for completion in early 1984.

By 1983, however, the PRG was facing increasing difficulties. Eastern Bloc aid proved something of a mixed blessing. The military and security forces benefited the most. By 1983 Grenada's People's Revolutionary Armed Forces (PRAF) outnumbered on their own the forces of all their Eastern Caribbean neighbours combined, and there were plans to expand them further in coming years. Cuba and Eastern Europe had done little for the country's economy, however. Most of their effort had been spent on improving Grenada's usefulness as a political and logistics base in the region. In addition, the heavy-handed advisors dispatched by Cuba had begun to antagonise the local population.

By the late summer of 1983, the NJM had split over the issue of the Communist connection. One faction, led by Bishop, was disappointed with progress and wanted closer ties with the West. A second, led by Deputy Prime Minister Bernard Coard, wanted to speed up the conversion to a Marxist state. The crisis came to a head on 13 October 1983, when Coard, having first obtained the backing of the military under Gen. Hudson Austin, ordered Bishop to step down from office. He was charged with failing to carry out the orders of the NJM's Central Committee, and placed under

Marine helicopter crewman mans a .50cal. Browning MG from the gunner's position of a CH-46D *Sea Knight*. He wears the Navy/Marine Corps SPH-3B helmet, PASGT body armour and standard CWU-27 flight suit. The heavy canvas gauntlets facilitate changing hot barrels, clearing jams, etc. (US Marine Corps)

house arrest. Several of his Ministers resigned in protest and were also arrested.

The Death of Bishop

The arrests were greeted with shock and anger by the population. Over the next several days large pro-Bishop demonstrations occurred throughout the island. There were reports of unrest in the militia, and a general strike was called in the capital, St George's. On Tuesday 18 October crowds of students surged through the city chanting pro-Bishop, anti-Coard slogans, watched impassively by police and soldiers.

In the midst of the crisis, Foreign Minister Unison Whiteman returned from New York, where he was scheduled to address the United Nations, and began agitating for Bishop's release. On the morning of 19 October Whiteman began addres-

sing a crowd in the streets of St George's. As the crowd swelled in numbers, the listeners decided to free Bishop themselves, and set out *en masse* for his official residence at Mount Royal. At first Bishop's guards stood their ground, even firing over the heads of the demonstrators; but in the end numbers prevailed and they finally allowed the crowd to free their prisoner.

After securing his release, Whiteman next persuaded Bishop to return with the crowd to St George's, where several of his Ministers were reportedly held at the 18th-century Fort Ruppert. Originally part of the harbour defences, the Fort was now used as a base for the People's Revolutionary Army. Another confrontation was avoided as the garrison, small and demoralised, gave up their arms to the crowd and permitted them to enter the Fort. While Bishop met with his chief supporters, the crowd continued to grow. At this point, PRA reinforcements arrived in the shape of three armoured personnel carriers and a truckload of soldiers.

After deploying in front of the Fort, the officer

US Army Ranger from 1/75th Ranger Bn. leads two handcuffed PRA infantrymen into captivity at Point Salines. Slung over his shoulder is one prisoner's folding stock AKM, and in his right hand he carries their web gear of Soviet origin. The captives wear Cuban fatigue uniforms and boots, while the helmets are the latest Soviet type. The large letters picked out in white rocks on the hillside read 'Siempre es 26' ('It is always 26'), a reference to the date (26 July) celebrated in Cuba as the official beginning of the revolution which placed Castro in power. (US Army)

cadet commanding the column gave the order to open fire. More than 100 Grenadians fell before the withering fire or were trampled in the ensuing panic.[1] 'Oh God, they have turned their guns on the masses', were Bishop's last recorded words. As survivors fled, the PRA moved quickly to re-arrest the leaders. Bishop, four of his Ministers and three prominent supporters were taken at once to an inner courtyard of the Fort. Shortly thereafter, they were put to death by the PRA. Education Minister Jacqueline Creft was beaten to death. Bishop, Whiteman and the others were shot as they knelt beside a basketball court. A 24-hour curfew was immediately imposed and notice was given that violators would be shot on sight.

[1]After giving the order to fire, the column commander, Officer Cadet Conrad Meyers, was himself shot dead by one of his own men, possibly by accident, along with two other soldiers.

The Decision for Intervention

On the night of 19 October Gen. Austin spoke on the radio, offering his own version of events, and announcing the formation of a 16-member Revolutionary Military Council with himself as head. No mention was made of Coard, who was rumoured to have fled. (He was in fact acting as Austin's advisor at the time.) Under cover of a four-day curfew, arrests of prominent citizens were carried out. Included were local businessmen, former Bishop officials, PRA officers and NJM cadres suspected of disloyalty. The bodies of Bishop and the other victims were taken from Fort Ruppert and secretly buried in a garbage pit at Calivigny Camp on the east coast of the island.

Meanwhile, the news of Bishop's death was received with shock and horror throughout the normally placid Eastern Caribbean. Even those governments critical of his policies had generally adopted a 'wait and see' attitude toward the NJM. Now it had all ended in bloodshed. Amid newspaper calls for a boycott or embargo against

US Army Military Police from the XVIII Airborne Corps' 16th MP Brigade take up positions outside Cuban dormitories at the enclave near Point Salines. They are relieving MPs from the 82nd Military Police Company (wearing the 'Fritz' helmets). The field MP brassard in muted colours can be seen on one policeman's left shoulder. (US Army)

Grenada, Caribbean leaders denounced the killings. Two meetings of regional organisations were hurriedly scheduled for the end of the week.

On Friday 21 October the leaders of six small nations forming the Organisation of Eastern Caribbean States met in Bridgetown, Barbados to consider collective action against Grenada. Under the chairmanship of Dominica's President Eugenia Charles, the six nations voted to intervene militarily to restore order to the region. As none of the six (Dominica, St Lucia, St Vincent, Montserrat, St Kitts-Nevis and Antigua) possessed the necessary forces, an appeal was made to non-member states Jamaica and Barbados, and to the United States. A formal request for assistance under Article 8 of the OECS Charter was presented on Sunday 23 October. In the meantime a series of sanctions against the RMC was announced. (The American Deputy Assistant Undersecretary for Caribbean Affairs attended the Friday meeting. Grenada, a member of OECS, did not bother to send a delegate.)

On Saturday 22nd a meeting of the CARICOM (Caribbean Community) States was held in Port of Spain, Trinidad. A majority of delegates supported the idea of intervention, if the RMC would not peacefully accept a CARICOM fact-finding commission and a Caribbean Peacekeeping Force. The meeting adjourned in the early hours of Sunday morning.

The United States had been closely monitoring developments in Grenada since the arrest of Bishop the week before. Of primary concern was the safety of American citizens on the island: in spite of the poor relations between the two countries, there were thought to be about 1,000 US citizens on Grenada. Most were students and faculty of St George's University Medical School, an American-run institution providing medical training to aspiring doctors unable to find places in US medical schools.

On the evening of Bishop's murder, 19 October, the Joint Chiefs of Staff issued a warning order for non-combatant evacuation to the Commander-in-Chief, Atlantic Fleet (CinClant), requesting possible courses of action. Early on the morning of the 20th the National Security Council's Special Situations Group met to recommend options to President Ronald Reagan. Planning continued all day Friday, but, with the request for assistance from the OECS, it took a different turn. A military option was now required.

The Forces

The sudden onset of the crisis severely curtailed the forces available for any proposed operation. Command arrangements would also have to be established. Happily, adequate naval forces were immediately available. Already at sea were ships of two Navy Task Forces, en route to a routine deployment in the Mediterranean. The first, Task Force 124, under Capt. Carl E. Erie, was built around the helicopter carrier (LPH) *Guam* and four landing ships of Amphibious Squadron Four. (These were designated PHIBRON FOUR in the Navy's curious terminology.) Embarked were 1,700 combat-ready Marines of the 22nd MAU (Marine Amphibious Unit) under Col. James P. Faulkner,

together with landing craft, tanks and amphibious tractors. The ground elements comprised Battalion Landing Team (BLT) 2/8 (2nd Battalion, 8th Marine Regiment), under Lt.Col. Ray L. Smith, and one artillery battery. *Guam* also carried the aircraft of Marine Medium Helicopter Squadron 261 (Reinforced)—HMM-261. They were the intended relief for sister units in 24th MAU then deployed at the Beirut International Airport, Lebanon, as part of the Multinational Peacekeeping Force. Also diverted from her routine transit was the *Independence* Carrier Battle Group, under R.Adm. Richard C. Berry. This comprised the *Independence* herself, her escort of cruisers and destroyers, and the aircraft of Carrier Air Wing 6 (CVW-6). Both forces had sailed for the Mediterranean on Tuesday 18 October, and were directed to steer closer to Grenada on Friday the 21st.

The original plan was to use these forces to

Military Police on guard outside the Cuban barracks at Point Salines. The M-60 machine gunner relaxing beneath the camouflage poncho liner is enjoying a snack of C-Ration peaches. Note the tripod-mounted M-60, rarely seen in the field: most M-60s are fired from the waist or bipod. (US Army)

conduct a routine evacuation of Americans from the island. The Navy and Marines were experienced in this sort of operation and the procedure was well established. With Marines providing security, the evacuees would be collected and convoyed to Pearls Airport. From there, they would be flown by helicopter to ships offshore and thence to Barbados. This plan, however, presupposed at least the acquiescence of the Grenadian authorities, a point now seriously in doubt. The US estimated there were between 1,200 and 1,500 members of the PRA and some 2,000 to 5,000 militia on the island, perhaps about to fight a civil war. There were also thought to be about 700 Cubans, whose status and instructions were unclear. Any of these groups might decide to interfere with the evacuation and place American lives in jeopardy.

Nevertheless, a non-combatant evacuation was still being planned as late as Friday 21 October, and the receipt of the OECS request. Although the final decision was not made by President Reagan until Saturday, warning orders were issued to selected units of the Army and Air Force in the United States on the evening of the 21st. Included were both of the crack Army Ranger battalions (one at Ft Stewart, Georgia the other at Ft Lewis, Washington); the Ready Brigade of the 82nd Airborne Division at Ft Bragg, North Carolina; and certain units of the 1st Special Operations Command. The Air Force alerted its 1st Special Operations Wing at Hurlburt Field, Florida and other transport units of the Military Airlift Command. The official orders to execute the Grenada mission, now named

Two NCOs from the 2/75th Ranger Bn. man an M224 60 mm Lightweight Company Mortar, on M8 Baseplate. Pushed into near-obsolescence in the early 1960s, the 60 mm Mortar came into its own during the Vietnam War, when US troops found the 81 mm mortar too unwieldy for use outside firebases. In December 1970 the M224 replaced the 81 mm in Airborne, Airmobile and Infantry units. Both men wear the Vietnam OD Jungle Fatigues. The Ranger on the left has fitted his canteens with M1 Drinking Device Caps, which allow use whilst wearing the M17 Protective Mask. The pistol in his M1916 holster appears to be the double-action Beretta M92 in 9 mm, recently tested by the US Army. The right hand man carries a Gerber Mk. 1 knife, with nylon-wrapped grip, in the grenade pocket of his magazine pouch. Note the strobe light and pilot's penlight attached to the right shoulder of his Y-harness. (US Army)

'Urgent Fury', were issued late on Saturday. D-Day was set for Tuesday 25 October, less than 48 hours away.

Prelude and Preparation

Meanwhile, on Grenada, the RMC met on Thursday 20 October to consider future actions. Among its concerns were the fear of invasion, and the necessity of reconciling the population to its seizure of power. The curfew was lifted briefly on Friday, so that people could shop for food. A sort of half-hearted apology was broadcast on Saturday, along with edited tapes of imprisoned Bishop supporters, apparently taking responsibility for the massacre. (The tapes were so poorly prepared that most listeners assumed the speakers to have been drugged or tortured, adding to the RMC's credibility problems.)

There was little the RMC could do about an invasion. They correctly assumed that their forces could deal with anything OECS and CARICOM could mount, but they were also aware of US naval forces in the vicinity. Their only hope lay with Cuba. After Bishop's murder the response of Havana was eagerly awaited. The Cubans were in a quandary. Bishop had been made into something of a hero in Cuba, yet they could not afford to jeopardise their investment in Grenada by denouncing his murderers. Their 20 October announcement was a compromise, yet it must have chilled its RMC listeners. The Cubans described the killings as 'atrocious acts', praised Bishop's memory, and called for 'exemplary punishment' for those responsible. Austin despatched a personal appeal to Fidel Castro on Friday. Citing the imminent threat of invasion, he asked for Cuban troops to fight under his command.

On Saturday 22 October Cuba's ambassador to Grenada delivered Castro's reply verbally to Austin. He began by lecturing the RMC at length, blaming them for the crisis. It would be 'unthinkable and impossible' to send Cuban forces to the island, certainly not to fight under Grenadian command. However, the honour of Cuba was at stake, and its status as the champion of Communist revolution in the Third World. Castro therefore offered the RMC the use of Cubans already on the island. Advisors to the PRA would fight with their units, and the Cuban workers at Point Salines would

Wednesday 26 October—during a lull in the fighting near St George's, a vigilant Marine radio operator phones in a Sitrep (Situation Report). He has fashioned a field-expedient assault sling for his M16A1 from a piece of clothesline. The AN/PRC-77 radio is contained within a special pocket in the ALICE rucksack. He carries an M67 fragmentation grenade looped to his harness, and a large pair of bolt cutters, the handles of which can be seen by his elbow. (USMC)

be responsible for its defence. (All work on the airport had been halted after Bishop's murder.) They would fight under Cuban command, not the PRAF's. Unspoken was Castro's worst-case hypothesis: if the United States was goaded into invading Grenada, might it not also one day intervene elsewhere, in Nicaragua perhaps, or even Cuba? The 'revolution without frontiers' in South and Central America might be in jeopardy.

The RMC had other visitors on Saturday. Pearls Airport, closed since Wednesday, was opened briefly to allow a chartered aircraft to land. It brought a delegation of British and American consular officials to evaluate conditions on the island and discuss a civilian evacuation. (Since Bishop's murder, there had been only sporadic telephone service off the island. Contact with the Medical School had been maintained by amateur shortwave radio operators at the school.) After driving around and interviewing some of their nationals, the officials met with a RMC major. Although he assured them that the airport would re-open on Monday, he was vague and obstructive, and the Americans felt he was stalling for time. The diplomats departed on Monday. The airport stayed closed to normal traffic.

Another consideration entered the political scene over the weekend: a letter from Governor-General Sir Paul Scoon. Scoon, the Queen's representative on the island, had largely ceremonial duties and had been quietly tolerated by the PRG. Kept a virtual prisoner at Government House, he smuggled out a letter after Bishop's death. It was a request for outside intervention to restore order, and for personal protection for himself and his staff. Since the United States did not recognise the RMC, they chose to regard Scoon as the highest legitimate authority on the island, and accepted the letter as an official request.

Sunday was a busy day for both sides. The RMC attempted anti-invasion preparations while still maintaining its curfew patrols. There was fear of arming the pro-Bishop militia, so they were left out of the RMC's plans. At Point Salines the Cubans were also busy. The contruction workers had been divided up into three provisional companies and issued heavy weapons from PRA stocks. (They already had their personal weapons, and had been carrying them since Wednesday.) All of the Cuban workers had at least militia training, and most of the younger ones were Army veterans or reservists. After blocking the incomplete runway with oil drums, stakes, construction equipment and barbed wire, they were set to work digging emplacements. Together with PRA troops, the Cubans would be responsible for beach defence, while the PRA proper would handle the anti-aircraft guns. The gunners were well trained: captured range cards and manuals later showed that they had been thoroughly instructed in American tactics and aircraft characteristics.

Also on Sunday 23 October V.Adm. Joseph Metcalf III, normally Commander, Second Fleet, arrived with his staff aboard *Guam* to assume command of newly activated Joint Task Force 120. His Deputy was Army Maj.Gen. H. Norman Schwarzkopf. They brought with them the results

The prototypical Marine of the 1980s, photographed at St George's on the invasion's second day. He wears the M1 Steel Helmet with Woodland cover, PASGT Vest and ALICE equipment over his BDU uniform. On his left thigh is the M17A1 Gas Mask in its container, behind which can be seen the standard US Navy flashlight, not often seen in the field. An AN/PRC-77 field radio is carried with his rucksack. (USMC)

of a JTF-120 planning session held at Norfolk on Saturday. A briefing was held in the carrier's crowded flag plot for Capt. Erie's staff. The mood was sombre. That morning, word had arrived of the attack on the Multinational Force in Lebanon. First reports were vague, but casualties were known to be heavy. The Marines were especially concerned: the unit attacked in Lebanon was their sister 24th MAU. Many of the casualties would be close personal friends.

The original plan for 'Urgent Fury' was loosely based on an exercise called 'Ocean Venture '81', held partially in the Caribbean two years previously. This envisioned the rescue of Americans taken hostage in a hostile Third World country. A force of Rangers, Marines and Paratroops were employed, assisted by Special Operations units.

The JTF-120 plan divided the island roughly in half, with the northern part allocated to the Navy and Marines, and the southern to the Army and Air Force. The first objective was to secure the students and the means for their evacuation. The situation was complicated by the Medical School's two campuses, with an unknown number of Americans at each.

On the morning of 25 October, after preliminary reconnaissance, the Marines would go ashore to secure Pearls Airport, using landing craft and helicopters. At the same time, Army Rangers would seize Point Salines Airport by *coup de main*. One company would land by parachute; the rest would come in by C-130 for an Entebbe-style attack, with armed jeeps rolling from taxiing aircraft. Several hours later, more C-130s would bring in a battalion of the 82nd Airborne Division to reinforce the Rangers. More paratroops would deploy to Barbados, where the government had made available its airport for their use. Then, together with Caribbean Peacekeeping Forces, they would deploy to Grenada.

At the time of the initial landings, three special missions would be executed. Two would be carried out by the Navy's *élite* special forces, the SEALs of SEAL Team Four. Raid 1 was to move to Government House, collect the Governor-General and take him to a 'safe-house' on the island (the home of a retired British officer) for safekeeping. Raid 2 was to destroy the 75-kilowatt transmitter of Radio Free Grenada. Raid 3 was the riskiest of all.

'Oh God, they have turned their guns on the masses!' Prime Minister Maurice Bishop and Gen. Hudson Austin, in happier days. At this time, the PRA were still wearing surplus American-style fatigues. (US State Department)

A unit of the counter-terrorist 'Delta Force' was to carry out a ground attack on the Richmond Hill Prison, supported by helicopters of the 101st Airborne Division (Air Assault). After these had neutralised the guards, Delta Force was to rescue the prisoners and secure them for evacuation. This mission was risky, since the prison was virtually surrounded by PRA installations, including Fort Frederick, the PRA Headquarters. Only the fear that the guards would massacre the prisoners justified its consideration at all.

Throughout Sunday and Monday, the sailors and Marines of JTF-120 went about their duties. Back in the United States, Rangers of both battalions carried out final preparations for their part in the operation at Hunter Army Airfield, Georgia. Because of the need to pre-position the special operations personnel, the SEALs and Delta Force members were parachuted on to the island during the night of 23/24 October, using HALO (High Altitude, Low Opening) techniques. Due to an equipment failure, one of the aircraft missed its

Rangers of the 2nd Bn. and one of their armed jeeps guard Cuban prisoners at Point Salines. Both men wear the commercial load-bearing vests donated to the unit by the manufacturer for field testing. The bewildering jumble of equipment strapped to the jeep includes packs, LAW anti-tank rockets and stretcher. The headlights and identification markings of the Ford M151A2 jeep have been covered over with tape. (US Army)

drop zone and several jumpers went into the water. Four Navy SEALs apparently became entangled in their parachutes and drowned in the surf.

On Monday 24 October, after a final meeting with the RMC, the American diplomats departed from Pearls Airport. Shortly afterwards a Cubana An-24 airliner landed. Aboard was Cuban Col. Pedro Tortolo Comas of the *Fuerzas Armadas Revolucionarias*. Tortolo, a graduate of the Soviet Frunze and Voroshilov military schools, was then serving as an Army-level Chief-of-Staff in Cuba. He was uniquely qualified for his Grenada assignment, since he had commanded the Cuban Military Mission to the island for several years. His immediate orders were to take charge of the Cubans on the island, oversee the defence preparations, and provide for non-combatants. He had 53 members of the Military Mission and 636 construction workers

available to fight. The remainder of the 784 Cubans on the island—advisors in agriculture, administration and medicine, etc.—were told to respect the curfew and stay indoors. About 50 Cuban dependants and women advisors were evacuated to the merchant vessel *Viet Nam Heroico*, anchored in St George's harbour.

There was also a final RMC attempt at diplomacy. Two successive telexes were sent to the Foreign and Commonwealth Office in London, formally requesting British help in forestalling the imminent invasion. Unfortunately, the RMC had an obsolete telex directory, and they were, in fact, addressing their pleas to a plastic bag manufacturer in London's West End. (The possibility of an armed intervention had first been mentioned to British diplomats in the Caribbean on Friday, by officials of the Barbados government, among others. Prime Minister Thatcher was officially notified on Monday 24 October by American Ambassador John Louis.)

The Navy also used Monday for some necessary preliminaries. The JTF-120 plan for 'Urgent Fury' left pre-invasion reconnaissance up to the individual services, the Navy in the north and the Army/Air Force team in the south. Each took a different approach; the Navy photographed Pearls Airport and other objectives on the afternoon of the 24th, but the Air Force decided to keep away from Point Salines until the last moment. (Ironically, the photos of Pearls were not especially significant, but if the Air Force had looked at Point Salines at the same time, they would have discovered the blocked runway twelve hours earlier.) The Navy had also ordered a ground reconnaissance of proposed landing areas. Further SEALs of Teams Four and Six arrived on the evening of the 24th. A C-9A transport brought them to Barbados where, watched by curious reporters, they transferred to three helicopters for the ride out to the ships. That night, they would be the first ashore.

On the second day of fighting in St George's, a Marine machine gun team pauses for a break. Readily identifiable as Marines from the small American flag shoulder patches, both men wear BDUs with standard black leather combat boots. Note the Marine Kabar fighting knife on the gunner's belt, and the extra M-60 belt carried at the assistant gunner's side, in a cardboard box below his gas mask carrier. (USMC)

The First Day: 25 October

The Reconnaissance

The night of 24/25 October was rainy with moderate surf. At about 10 pm, several parties of SEALs landed from rubber Sea Fox raiding boats on the north-east coast of Grenada, where the Navy expected to conduct its surface and helicopter assault the next day. The SEALs' mission was to reconnoitre landing beaches, then infiltrate inland and check out Pearls Airport and its defences. The mission was successfully executed, but the report they sent back at 3 am was bad. There were reefs fringing the landing beaches, impassable for landing craft, and probably for amtracks (amphibious armoured personnel carriers) as well. The airport itself was well defended by troops and anti-aircraft guns. The SEALs had been close enough to overhear conversations, as the PRA defenders discussed the situation. The consensus seemed to be that the US would not invade and the alert was a waste of time.

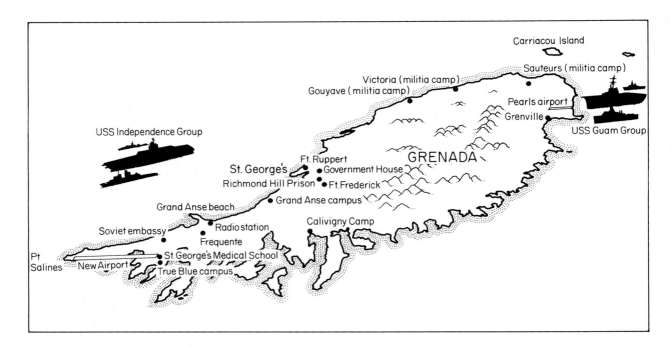

At about the same moment as the SEALs reported back, a single Air Force AC-130 Spectre was closing the southern tip of the island. Refuelled in flight from KC-135 tankers, this gunship of the 16th Special Operations Squadron, 1st Special Operations Wing had flown non-stop from Hurlburt Field, Florida. It was equipped with infrared sensors and low-light television cameras, so sensitive that crews often used them to track alligator poachers in the Florida Everglades. Its mission on 25 October was to reconnoitre Point Salines airfield for the MC-130 transports carrying the Rangers, two hours behind them in flight. The first look at the runway was enough; it was blocked with vehicles, obstacles and construction equipment. This information was relayed at once to the following aircraft, and the AC-130 crew settled down to wait.

On board the troop-laden MC-130 *Combat Talon* transports, the Ranger commanders hurriedly conferred with Air Force counterparts. The plan for a limited drop by only one company was scrapped. Everyone from both Ranger battalions would now jump (excepting only vehicle drivers) along with an Air Force Combat Control Team, needed to direct C-130 landing operations. The word was quickly passed to the men to begin in-flight rigging of their parachutes. Restricted by the jeeps and other equipment, the Rangers had no room to conduct

normal 'station-rigging' and resorted instead to the 'buddy system', helping each other assemble and check their equipment. Machine guns and mortars were hurriedly unfastened from vehicles, loaded into weapons containers, and attached to jump harnesses. Rifles and grenade launchers were clipped on by snap-links, and rucksacks ripped apart and repacked with only grenades, ammunition and water. Normal jump procedures were abandoned. The men were told they would jump from minimum altitude with very heavy loads. The 2/75th's commander, Lt.Col. Ralph Hagler, decided his men would also forego reserve 'chutes: they could do without the weight, and, in case of malfunction, there would be no time for a reserve to deploy anyway. Non-jump personnel were pressed into service as 'jump safeties', and, if qualified, jumpmasters. The hasty preparations caused by this change of plan at least had the virtue of preventing any anxiety among the troops, few of whom had ever been in combat. Many men were still making last-minute adjustments to their equipment even as they approached the drop zone.

Reveille came early aboard the warships. Even as crews aboard the *Guam* were going to flight quarters, in the crowded flag plot Adm. Metcalf was revising his own plans in light of the SEAL report. The proposed beach landing by one Marine company was cancelled, and the troops aboard the

LST *Manitowoc* were stood down. One of the two helicopter landing zones was also moved 700 metres south of the airfield, to keep clear of the anti-aircraft defences. On the flight deck, two Marine companies filed aboard HMM-261's CH-46s in the rain-swept darkness. Shortly before the scheduled H-hour of 0500, the *Guam* began launching her helos.

Grenville and Pearls—The Marine Landings

After take-off, the CH-46s formed a loose column of three aircraft sections and headed in, led by two armed AH-1T *SeaCobras* of HML-167. Two more *Cobras* brought up the rear. The force headed inland following a rain squall, and touched down at daybreak, 0520 hours. As the lead CH-46 came out of the rain it drew fire from several 12.7 mm anti-aircraft guns. There were no casualties, and the escorting *Cobras* quickly suppressed the guns. Then the Marines of Company E, 2/8th Marines moved out to secure the airfield. Simultaneously, a second assault by Co. F, 2/8 was being made into LZ 'ORIOLE', near Grenville, south of Pearls. It was unopposed except for some inaccurate mortar fire. Both objectives, the airport and the second largest town, were secured by 0630 hours. Col. Tortolo's aircraft and another small airliner were also secured. In spite of their preparations, the speed and power of the assault came as a shock to the defenders, most of whom elected to surrender rather than resist. This was helpful, as throughout the operation the Marines had orders to keep casualties on both sides to a minimum.

Dawn at Salines

As the first Marines landed to secure Pearls Airport, the C-130s carrying the Rangers were approaching the island from the south, flying low to avoid possible radar detection. As they approached the drop zone the aircraft swung into a trail formation. Leading was Air Force Col. Hugh Hunter's lizard-painted *Spectre*. Behind him, strung out in line, were the 8th SOS aircraft carrying the 1/75th contingent, and then a 'cell' of two more AC-130s. Bringing up the rear were more MC-130s with 2/75th, making a total of 13 aircraft, including the three gunships. As they approached the island, the jumpmasters ordered the Rangers to their feet. Above the roar of the engines, they could hear the anti-aircraft guns open fire.

A recon trooper from 1st Sqn. (Air), 17th Cavalry of the 82nd Airborne starts his motorcycle at Point Salines. These bikes provide essential cross-country speed and mobility, but are, in spite of special mufflers, exceedingly noisy. In Grenada they were used for reconnoitring the poorly surfaced country lanes in the interior of the island. The stock and handguards of this man's M-16 have been camouflaged with green tape, cut into a disruptive pattern. Also note the pilot's penlight taped to his harness on the right side. (US Army)

The defenders had been taken by surprise, but reacted swiftly. A heavy volume of fire was opened on the lead aircraft. Col. Hunter had expected some opposition, but the strength of the defences was a shock: 'I was surprised with the weapons they used. I didn't anticipate as much triple-A [anti-aircraft artillery] fire as we received.' Responsible for the success of the landing, as well as his own personnel and equipment, Hunter made a quick decision. He would abort the original jump and allow the two gunships in the middle of the formation to 'hose down' the defences first. He also reversed the order of the jump; 2/75th would now go in first, while the aircraft with 1/75th made a circle of the airfield and came in behind them. As the transports overflew the DZ, the first two received the abort; but on the

On board the LPH *Guam,* one of the two surviving AH-1T *Sea Cobras* of HML-167 is refuelled by maintenance crews. Throughout the operation the ships' crews worked tirelessly to support air and ground operations, while maintaining a tight blockade around the island. (US Navy)

third, carrying the 1/75th command group, the jump lights unaccountably turned green, and Lt.Col. Wesley B. Taylor and 30 of his men were out the doors before anyone realised the mistake. (On this mission, to minimise their exit time, the Rangers were using a 'shotgun' technique of jumping from both doors of the aircraft.) Momentarily nonplussed to find himself virtually alone under his canopy, Taylor nevertheless recovered quickly and, on landing, he and his battalion sergeant-major divided up the men and went into action.

Meanwhile, the *Spectres* had taken on the anti-aircraft guns. The enemy gunners were well trained and stubbornly stood by their pieces, actually scoring hits on both gunships and some of the troop carriers. The AC-130s were armed with 20 mm, 40 mm and 105 mm cannon, and, as the 23 mm anti-aircraft guns had an effective range of only 6,600 feet, the *Spectre* crews were able to use all of them. The 20 mm Vulcan guns were especially effective.

'The . . . 2,500 rounds a minute [rate of fire] really cleared the crews from the anti-aircraft guns,' said one crewman. By 0615 hrs (45 minutes later than planned) ground fire had slackened considerably and the *Talons* swung in toward the DZ once again. This time, an even lower approach was specified. Col. Hunter knew from analysis of target photos that the anti-aircraft weapons, sited on a ridgeline overlooking the airfield, could not be depressed to fire at targets below 600 feet. The aircraft would go in at 500 feet.

From the door of the lead aircraft, Ranger Lt.Col. Ralph Hagler, commanding the 2nd Bn., observed anti-aircraft fire and Cuban mortar rounds impacting west of the airstrip. He turned and shouted to his men: 'Rangers, be hard!'—and then they were jumping. Col. Hagler was the first out; in 21 seconds, 250 Rangers were in the air with him. Conditions were far from ideal: the 20-knot ground winds were well above peacetime safety limits, and the DZ was narrow and bordered with water on both sides. Nevertheless, there was only one jump injury (a broken leg) and only one man went into the water (he swam ashore, even saving his equipment). Two men got 'hung up' as they jumped, and had to be pulled back inside the aircraft by Air Force jumpmasters.

Once on the ground, the Rangers quickly assembled and moved out, supported by Navy A-7 attack planes and the AC-130 gunships. It was immediately apparent that the Cubans had made a serious error in their deployments. Not anticipating an airborne landing, they had left only one company guarding the airstrip. Two others, along with PRA units, were dug in along the beach to oppose a seaborne attack. Some low hills also screened the Rangers from the anti-aircraft positions. The first objective was to clear the runway. It had been blocked with metal spikes driven into the tarmac, and with 55 gallon drums, barbed wire barricades and construction equipment. As some men dragged away the drums and wire, other ingenious soldiers 'hot wired' some Cuban bulldozers that had been left in place, and used them to help. Another Ranger commandeered a steam roller and, harassed by sniper fire, drove it up and down the runway, pushing the spikes deep into the ground—it was the first time he'd ever

driven such a machine. By 0630 hrs, the runway was clear.

Next, the Rangers moved against the Cuban camp, first driving in its outposts. B Co., 1/75th started rolling up the Cuban flank from west to east at 0700 hours. Company First Sergeant Richard B. Caton led a three-man team against a Cuban position, killing two Cubans and capturing 28 more. Another team captured 17, and 15 weapons, including an RPK machine gun. Ranger snipers brought Cuban mortar positions under fire at ranges of 600–1,000 metres, and killed or wounded 18 Cubans from among the crews. Meanwhile A Co., 1/75th was attacking from east to west, using a captured bulldozer as a 'tank'. A Cuban-manned ZPU anti-aircraft gun was also captured, then turned around and used to bring the camp under fire. The Rangers considered an air strike on the position, but instead, Sgt. Caton sent a Cuban

Marine UH-1N and CH-46 helicopters are refuelled on board the *Guam* as Marine maintenance crews look on. In keeping with the tradition that 'every Marine is a rifleman', their standard duty uniform is BDU utilities, here worn with HGU-25/P cranial helmets and goggles for eye protection. (US Navy)

prisoner into the camp with instructions for them to surrender in 15 minutes 'or else'. About 175 Cubans chose to do so, and the position was taken. Several Cubans escaped, including Col. Tortolo, who managed to make his way to the Russian Embassy, where he was later awarded diplomatic status and returned to Cuba.

As the Rangers secured the camp, they soon encountered part of the Cuban force assigned to beach defence. As one of the Cuban companies attempted to withdraw, it ran into major elements of the 1/75th, and was sharply defeated in a brief fire-fight. Shortly thereafter the Rangers decided to push out a large movement-to-contact to clear the eastern end of the airstrip. As the Rangers moved out, the 2/75th was hit by the Cubans' most ambitious attack, this time led by three BTR-60

armoured personnel carriers. The attack was a disaster: anti-tank gunners immediately hit two APCs with recoilless rifle fire, then everyone else joined in with LAW (Light Anti-tank Weapon) rockets and small arms. The third APC attempted to flee, but was hit by a *Spectre* gunship and then by more anti-tank rounds. Aside from snipers, who would continue to trouble the Americans for days, this attack put an end to resistance at Point Salines. By mid-morning the runway was open, and MC-130s brought in the Rangers' jeeps and equipment and began taking out wounded. A message was despatched to Pope Air Force Base, North Carolina to begin flying in the 82nd Airborne troops.

Special Operations

None of the Special Operations went exactly as planned. Raid 2, the SEAL attack on Radio Free Grenada, came off the best. RFG had gone on the air at the first reports of landings, calling for militia mobilisation and for medical personnel to report for duty. The SEALs got into the transmitter compound late, and then experienced difficulty in

82nd Airborne company commander struggles with congested radio nets on his PRC-77 at Point Salines. The soldier looking on wears the new PASGT 'Fritz' helmet, made of 19 layers of Kevlar ballistic cloth. Stuck in the retaining band is a stripper clip guide, used in refilling M-16 magazines. In the background, Rangers of the 1st Bn. move out toward their next objective. (US Army)

C-130 *Hercules* **transport of the 317th Military Airlift Wing, from Pope AFB, taxies past the control tower at Point Salines and a variety of captured vehicles. In several versions, the performance of this outstanding aircraft was a major factor in the success of 'Urgent Fury'. (US Air Force)**

shutting it down. RFG finally went off the air in the midst of martial exhortations about 0615 hours.

Raid 3, the Delta Force attack on Richmond Hill Prison, had been timed to coincide with the Point Salines jump. The ground component was ready, and the supporting 101st helicopters lifted off from the *Guam* on schedule. However, the 45 minute delay at the airport proved fatal. By the time word came to proceed, it was far too late: the anti-aircraft defences were fully alert, and the initial helicopter attack was met with withering fire. At least one UH-60 was shot down, and probably one Hughes 500 as well. One 101st pilot was killed and six aircrewmen were wounded. Cautiously watching from his cell, imprisoned Grenadian journalist Allister Hughes saw the aircraft driven off, and heard guards boast of downing two 'MiGs'. With the prison surrounded by PRA troops, it was obvious that further efforts would only endanger the prisoners, and the attack was abandoned.

Raid 1, the rescue of the Governor-General, also got off to a bad start. The rescue force, 22 Navy SEALs, came under fire as they assaulted the grounds of Government House on the outskirts of St George's. Inside, they found Scoon and members of his staff. Optimistically, a 'Welcome, US Marines' sign had been placed on the front lawn. Plans for exfiltration were quickly abandoned. After a brief exchange of fire, the PRA commander sent for reinforcements, including three armoured personnel carriers.

Fort Frederick

The plight of the trapped SEAL team quickly became a prime concern for Adm. Metcalf. His first action was to provide air cover in the form of AC-130s and Marine helicopter gunships. Unfortunately, Government House was also situated within range of anti-aircraft positions at Forts Frederick and Ruppert.

First to arrive were two Marine AH-1T *Cobras*, scrambled from the *Guam* to work over the anti-aircraft defences with cannon and TOW guided missiles. Anti-aircraft fire was heavy, from both multiple SU-23s and a BTR armoured vehicle. Enthusiastic PRA troops also added small arms fire. With their target's green-painted roofs concealing the tracers, the *Cobras* swung into the attack. The first machine was struck as it paused to guide in a TOW missile. The pilot, Marine Capt. Tim Howard, lost his right arm to a 23 mm cannon round, and further hits disabled his aircraft. Howard struggled with the controls, and managed to crash-land on a soccer field in the middle of St George's. His weapons controller, Capt. Jeb Seagle, himself injured in the crash, dragged the wounded pilot from the wreckage, only to be shot dead as he tried to signal the remaining aircraft.

'Before this happened, I never thought much about the military. Now, I never want to hear anyone say anything bad about the US armed forces again!' Medical students awaiting evacuation pose with an 82nd Airborne sergeant. Note that one of the students still wears the white armbands they were instructed to put on by radio. The sergeant's M17A1 Gas Mask Carrier has been secured shut by a strip of cloth, a normal pre-jump procedure. (US Army)

The second *Cobra* radioed for a CH-46 medevac and, together with an Air Force AC-130, escorted it in. The big transport helicopter touched down and, under fire, the crew chief jumped out and dragged Howard aboard. As it lifted off, the remaining *SeaCobra* continued to provide covering fire, only to be hit in its turn by cannon fire and shot down in the harbour. Both crewmen were killed. Capt. Seagle's body was recovered by PRA troops and taken to a nearby funeral parlour. When its owner refused to admit them (his facilities were already overtaxed with victims of the Fort Ruppert massacre), the body was left on the beach, where it was eventually found by American newsmen.

The PRA next launched their own attack on the SEALs, led by the three BTRs. Having no anti-tank weapons, the SEALs called in an AC-130, which destroyed one vehicle and stopped all the rest. An uneasy stand-off followed, finally broken by a telephone call from the island's police chief to Governor-General Scoon. He asked how many Americans there were and if they were well armed. 'I've never seen so many guns in my life,' lied Scoon. (The SEALs had not come equipped for a siege.) The PRA decided to content themselves by surrounding the house.

After the loss of the *Cobras*, Metcalf ordered a full-scale attack on the St George's defences by A-7s from *Independence*. The air strikes did a fair amount of damage to both forts, killing the anti-aircraft commander at Fort Ruppert, among others. Unhappily, they also hit adjacent Fort Matthew, now converted to use as a mental hospital. (It was identically painted to the nearby military installations and a PRA flag had been raised in front by Grenadian soldiers.) A number of patients were killed and, for the next several days, escaped mental patients could be found wandering around the capital. As darkness came to St George's, blacked out by a power failure unrelated to the invasion, PRA morale was still high. They had defeated two American attacks and still had the SEALs surrounded. The soldiers also boasted inaccurately of Cuban successes at Point Salines.

The 82nd Arrives

The first contingent of paratroops was airborne from Pope AFB shortly after 1000 hrs, and touched down at Point Salines at 1405 hours. The initial contingent included Maj.Gen. Edward L. Trobaugh, the 82nd's commander, a Forward Command Post and one rifle company of 2/325th Infantry. The rest of the battalion came in over the next four hours, along with contingents from the Caribbean Peacekeeping Force. Operations from the airstrip were difficult. Only some 5,000 feet of the runway was usable and there was no ramp area, requiring the aircraft to be unloaded on the runway. The usual procedure was to land a C-141 and start unloading, then land a C-130 behind it. It was slow work, and as many as five aircraft orbited overhead awaiting their turn. Snipers harassed the unloading.

Even after the arrival of reinforcements, it took

several hours to secure the hundreds of prisoners and the perimeter itself. In the late afternoon a contingent from both Ranger battalions secured the True Blue campus of the Medical School and cleared a landing zone in the school's basketball court. While most of the students awaited evacuation, the school's staff and senior students pitched in to help the Army medics with casualties. Intelligence officers interviewed other students for information on Grand Anse, the second campus. There was an embarrassing lack of information about the island and, until PRA maps captured at Point Salines could be copied, troops made do with photocopied tourist ones.

During the night, survivors of the Cuban forces and PRA troops regrouped north of the airfield. Others harassed the Americans, who called down AC-130s on them with great effect. Six 105 mm artillery pieces also arrived during the night, along with the headquarters of the 82nd's 2nd Brigade. Adding to security problems, the 82nd found itself

These BTR-60PBs, of which eight were supplied by the Soviet Union to the PRA, were among six destroyed by US forces. Two BRDM-2s were also supplied, one of which was destroyed. (US Army)

custodian of several hundred Grenadian refugees. To their surprise, the Americans found themselves greeted as liberators, and many of the refugees had brought gifts of food to present to them.

The Second Day: 26 October

The Relief of the SEALs

Metcalf's most immediate problem for the second day was getting a relief force to Government House. His Deputy, Gen. Schwarzkopf, suggested using the Marine Company aboard LST *Manitowoc*, which had been 'scratched' from the Pearls landing and was available. Metcalf agreed and shifted the boundaries of his forces, assigning St George's to the Marines. By a happy coincidence, one of **PHIBRON FOUR**'s staff officers was an amateur small boat sailor who had experience of the island's coastline. He quickly pinpointed Grand Mal Bay, a few hundred yards north of the city, as a suitable landing place. Metcalf ordered the Navy task force to proceed around the island and effect a landing operation. Until this could be done, the SEALs would depend on the AC-130s for support.

The Grand Mal landing was made in two parts. First, Co. F, 2/8 Marines assembled at LZ 'ORIOLE', Grenville for a night-time, cross-island helicopter assault. At 0300 hrs, D + 1, they were inserted into LZ 'FUEL', adjacent to Grand Mal. At 0400 hrs, Co. G, 2/8 came ashore in 13 amtracks, along with five M60A1 tanks from LSD *Fort Snelling*. Under command of Lt.Col. Ray Smith, commander of 2/8, the force assembled and moved out for Government House. Both besieged and besiegers had passed an anxious night. By dawn the PRA had become more aware of its actual situation. The Marine attack met little resistance. A BRDM was destroyed by an M60A1 tank, and the rest of the force faded away. The SEALs were relieved at 0700 hrs and, with the Governor-General and his staff, removed to the *Guam*.

Afterwards, Co. F, supported by armour and anti-tank elements, and assisted by the BLT's Reconnaissance Platoon, attacked south and occupied the Queen's Park Race Course, where they established a helicopter landing zone. On the way the Marines picked up a large quantity of abandoned weapons, including recoilless rifles, SU-23 and ZPU-4 anti-aircraft guns and small arms. Encouraged by the lack of opposition, Smith obtained permission to push on toward Fort Frederick with both of his rifle companies, and this was secured by 1700 hours. At the fort, in addition to further quantities of weapons, a large store of documents was found. Some of the captured documents seemed to indicate that there might be some 1,700 Cubans on the island. This information was relayed to the Army. (Unhappily, it later proved to be incorrect.) The Recon Platoon seized

adjacent Fort George, also a PRA base, late in the day.

Rescue at Grand Anse

Metcalf's second problem on Wednesday was securing the 200-plus students known to be at the Grand Anse campus south of St George's. A joint heliborne operation was decided upon, using Army Rangers and Marine helicopters from the *Guam*. Since the invasion on Monday the only contact with the students had been by shortwave radio. Although the Cuban/PRA force had left the students alone, they had occupied buildings adjoining the campus and these had been the targets of US air strikes. The students were advised by radio to be ready for evacuation.

At about 1630 hrs, one of the students took a look outside and saw 'something right out of "Apocalypse Now"'—a line of helicopters headed straight in from the bay. Anti-aircraft fire claimed one

US Navy SEALs in training, wearing the standard combat dress of Woodland-pattern cotton utilities and hat. Over this, they wear normal load-bearing equipment and SRU-21P Survival Vests. Originally intended for pilots, it is used to carry a variety of survival and special mission equipment. A pistol holster and combat knife are generally attached to the mesh body. (US Navy)

Marine CH-46, which crashed in the water just short of the beach. The pilot lowered the tail ramp, and the Rangers inside splashed into the surf to shelter behind the aircraft. Navy A-6s and A-7s and the ever-present AC-130s moved in to suppress the anti-aircraft guns. The campus was surrounded by several beachfront hotels, now occupied by the PRA. For 15 minutes the aircraft brought them under fire; then the Rangers rushed the buildings. Students in one dormitory first learned that they were rescued when a Ranger kicked in the door to their room and shouted 'US soldier, freeze! Friend or foe?'

'Friend,' they replied.

'Okay,' he said, 'just stay down.'

'They rescued us, they guarded us, they took us to safety,' said another student; 'they were wonderful.' In groups of forty, the students were led outside and loaded aboard the helicopters. With the loss of the CH-46 the rescue force was 12 seats short, so 12 Rangers volunteered to stay behind. After the departure of the rescue force they evaded PRA elements, stole a fishing boat and headed out to sea, where they were rescued by the destroyer *Caron*.

The 82nd Moves North

At Point Salines, much of the day was taken up in unloading aircraft. A second battalion (1/505th) came in early in the day, and then the first of the students evacuated from True Blue were taken aboard. As the women students filed aboard they paused to kiss the paratroops. To take some of the pressure off Salines, much of the logistical build-up went to Barbados, whose airport could take C-5A *Galaxys*. Among the items delivered on Wednesday were a company of UH-60 *Black Hawk* helicopters from the 82nd Combat Aviation Battalion.

On Wednesday afternoon the troops of the 2nd ('Falcon') Brigade attacked east of the airfield, toward a complex of warehouses adjoining the field. Sixteen Cubans were killed and 86 captured. The fight was going out of the Cubans. On the first day US radio monitors picked up a message addressed to Havana, requesting permission to surrender. 'No,' was the response, 'defend your positions.' A second message was intercepted that night, repeating the request. Again, the response was the same: 'For the glory of the Revolution, no.' In the warehouses, US troops found large caches of weapons—small arms, mortars, recoilless rifles and anti-aircraft guns. Some were obsolete weapons dating from Gairy's old Defence Force, but the rest seemed far in excess of even the expanded PRA's needs. Also discovered were thousands of uniforms, boots and every sort of military equipment. Ominously, there was also a large supply of prison uniforms.

At 0300 hrs on the 27th, the first flight of 21 helicopters took off from Barbados for the 130-mile overwater flight to Grenada. It included UH-60s of both the 82nd CAB and the 57th Medical Detachment, XVIII Airborne Corps. The remaining aircraft were single-engined OH-58 *Kiowa* and UH-1 *Iroquois* aircraft, which required escort for the long, night-time, overwater mission. The aircraft touched down at Salines at 0530 hrs, only to discover that the 10,000 gallon fuel bladder which they expected to find was empty. The UH-60s were immediately pressed into service hauling smaller 500 gallon bladders to and from the *Guam* to the airfield. The three 57th helicopters were split between Pearls and Salines, and began ferrying casualties out to the ships. Because of fuel shortages, it was decided to leave the remaining Army aircraft on Barbados for the time being. Air support was left to the Air Force *Spectres*, the Navy A-7s and the two surviving Marine *Cobras*.

The Third Day: 27 October

Missions scheduled for D+2 included continued Army operations north from Point Salines, while the Marines moved to secure key terrain in St George's. At Pearls, Co. E, 2/8th Marines moved out to capture the Mt Horne Agricultural Station, recovering large quantities of abandoned PRA weapons. The airport, meanwhile, had been re-opened under a new name: 'MCAS Douglass'—Marine Corps Air Station Douglass, named in honour of the 8th Marines' popular Sgt.Maj. F. B. Douglass, killed in the Beirut bombing.

Frequente

While a third battalion (1/508th) of their brigade came in by air, the 'Falcons' continued their push north from Salines, starting with an attack on the Police Academy at Grand Anse. Resistance for most

During the final days of the invasion, XVIII Airborne Corps troops crowd aboard a UH-60A *Blackhawk* at Point Salines. This aircraft is slowly replacing the venerable 'Huey' UH-1D and N as the standard troop carrier. Its combat debut on Grenada was very satisfactory. It proved to be a fast, tough ship, one aircraft taking over 40 hits from a variety of weapons but completing its mission and returning to be repaired. (US Army)

1: Delta Force, SOC
2: US Army Ranger, 2/75th Ranger Bn.
3: USAF AC-130 'Spectre' crewman

A

B

1: USMC machine gunner, 2/8th Marines, 22nd MAU
2: US Navy SEAL, SEAL Team Four
3: USMC rifleman, 2/8th Marines, 22nd MAU

C

1: US Army grenadier, 2/325th Inf. (Airborne),
   82nd Airborne Div.
2: US Army 'Dragon' A/T gunner, 2/505th Inf. (Airborne),
   82nd Airborne Div.
3: US Army sniper, 1/508th Inf. (Airborne), 82nd Airborne Div.

D

1: Private 1st Class, Grenada PRA
2: Armour crewman, Grenada PRA
3: Cuban construction worker

E

1: Teniente, Cuban FAR, advisor to PRA
2: Captain, Soviet Spetsnaz, advisor to PRA
3: PRM militiawoman, Rapid Mobilisation Co.

F

1: Private, Barbados Defence Force, Caribbean PKF
2: Private, 2nd Bn., Jamaica Regt., Caribbean PKF
3: Constable, Royal Barbados Police, Caribbean PKF
4: Military Policewoman, 16th MP Bde., US XVIII Abn. Corps

G

1: US Navy A-7 pilot, VA-15, USS Independence
2: USMC AH-1T pilot, HMM-261
3: US Army UH-60 pilot, 82nd Combat Aviation Bn.

1   2   3

of the day was limited to snipers. By this time many Cubans and PRA soldiers were discarding their weapons and uniforms, and attempting to blend into the civilian population. For their part, the civilians were not anxious to help them. The ordinary Grenadian people had resented the Cubans for years, and recent events had alienated the PRA from the populace. The Americans had come expecting a sullen and hostile population at best; instead they found themselves greeted everywhere as liberators. At first suspicious, then wary, and finally embarrassed at their reception, they continued operations amid scenes reminiscent of the liberation of Europe on a miniature scale. As soon as fighting was halted in any area, crowds gathered to cheer the Americans and offer gifts of food, water and cold drinks. The civilians cheered the air strikes, cheered their liberators, and shouted invective at the Cubans. An old woman stopped one Paratroop officer and cautioned him not to kill all

the Cubans: 'You must leave us one so we can execute him ourselves,' she insisted. Better than the cheers and cans of soda they provided, the Grenadian civilians enthusiastically led the Americans to arms caches, pointed out PRA men in civilian clothes, and provided every sort of intelligence information.

By afternoon, the 2nd Brigade were pushing through Frequente's Ruth Howard housing area and a section known as the Drive-In. A Navy A-7 air strike was called in by a Marine ANGLICO (Air, Naval Gunfire Liaison Company) officer attached to the 82nd. In a tragic accident, he mis-identified the target to the Navy jets, and one

Two Rangers from the 2nd Bn. examine Soviet AKMs and an RPD light machine gun discovered in the hills near Point Salines. Note the commercial vest worn by the Ranger on the right. The pockets contain 30-round M-16 magazines. Both men wear the Vietnam-vintage OD Jungle Fatigues. The special 'Ranger crush' of the M1951 Patrol Cap is also shown to advantage. (US Army)

33

On 28 October, Rangers from Co. A, 1st Bn. awaiting transport back to Ft Stewart, Georgia shield their ears as an Air Force C-141 takes off from Point Salines. Note the nametapes and 'catseye' markings at the back of their headgear, and the M-21 sniper rifle held by the Ranger in the centre. (US Army)

aircraft strafed a group of 82nd paratroops setting up a tactical command post amid some former Cuban barracks. The attack wounded 16 soldiers, one of whom later died.

The Calivigny Camp

While overseeing the 2nd Brigade operation, the main concern of the 82nd's Headquarters on Thursday was co-ordinating an airmobile assault to the east of the airfield. The objective was the Calivigny Barracks, a PRA installation thought to be defended by up to 600 Cuban and PRA soldiers and six anti-aircraft guns. The forces employed were one company of the 1/75th and the whole of 2/75th Rangers, loaded into eight 82nd CAB UH-60 *Blackhawks*. The briefing was hurried and grim: 'We all thought it was a suicide mission,' commented one pilot later.

The attack was launched about 1645 hrs, after extensive artillery and naval gunfire preparation (later found to be ineffective, since only one round landed in the compound). Just before the Rangers went in, Navy jets also put in an attack. The eight *Blackhawks* formed two flights of four, staying low to avoid possible anti-aircraft fire. The first two aircraft, Chalk One and Two, landed safely and their troops deployed. Chalk Three, however, was hit in the tail rotor as it landed, and swung into Chalk Two already on the ground. Both sets of rotors came apart in a flurry of broken blades. Behind them, Chalk Four swung sharply left to avoid the debris, struck the ground hard, and

snapped off its own tail. As the pilot tried to lift off, his damaged machine flipped over into the deploying Rangers. Three men were killed in this incident, and 12 others injured.

The remaining four *Blackhawks* landed safely, and the Rangers secured the camp in 15 minutes. The defenders, who turned out to number no more than 30, put up a good fight. One of the other *Blackhawks* was badly shot up, but managed to limp out to the *Guam*, its pilot and four crewmen wounded, its flight instruments gone and 45 bullet holes in fuel tanks, rotors and cabin. Only two UH-60s escaped damage, and an escorting OH-58 was also badly shot up. The mission, already expensive in men and hardware, would suffer further loss. After the action, the Army requested a Marine CH-53 *Sea Stallion* to recover the downed Army aircraft. On the first run the Marine pilot misjudged the weight of the *Blackhawk* and ended up dropping it. He then flew out to sea, dumped fuel and ammunition, and came back for a second load. This time a cargo strap broke, and a second Army *Blackhawk* smashed to earth with a broken back. The remaining aircraft were recovered without incident, but both dropped machines ended up as total write-offs.

The End in St George's

Before moving into St George's proper the Marines received reinforcements in the shape of H Battery, 3/10th Marines. Normally the MAU's artillery element, they were put ashore at Grand Mal to fight as a provisional rifle company. They moved quickly to LZ 'RACETRACK' to secure the command group and POW compound, while Co. F led the way into St George's. By then there was no resistance, only scattered bands of looters wandering the streets. Co. G reached the Richmond Hill Prison at about 1000 hrs, but found only four prisoners inside. The guards had taken off during the night and the prisoners had freed themselves and escaped. The Botanical Gardens, Belmont and finally Fort Ruppert were secured. The fort was deserted, its doors open. Two anti-aircraft guns sat abandoned behind the 18th-century battlements; beside them lay the body of a PRA officer. So many discarded weapons were found in one storeroom that a squad had to be left to guard them.

Final Operations

On D + 3, Army troops swept through the Lance aux Epines area and evacuated another 202 medical students, finally linking up with the Marines at St George's. At Pearls, Co. E, 2/8th fought the last action against an organised enemy force, ambushing a PRA squad north of the airport. Operations continued on D + 4 and D + 5, clearing the areas on the northern and eastern coasts. On Saturday 29 October, Caribbean Peacekeeping Force troops assumed control of Pearls Airport. At St George's, Marines of H Battery captured Bernard Coard and several other prominent NJM leaders, while 82nd paratroops took Gen. Austin and his bodyguards into custody. Together with members of the RMC, they were flown out to the *Guam* and placed in the ship's brig for safekeeping. With the lifting of the curfew, ordinary Grenadians came out in St George's to offer information, share food, or just talk or shake hands with the troops.

More 82nd units came in to replace the Rangers and Marines, who had orders to backload out for other missions. The Rangers returned to their home stations, while the Marines carried out a final amphibious operation on Monday on the island of Carriacou, north of Grenada. No resistance was encountered, and a large supply of arms was captured. The Marines turned over all responsibilities on Grenada to the 82nd Airborne Division and the Caribbean PKF, and departed for the Middle East on 2 November. Under orders from Governor-General Scoon, the 82nd arranged for the evacuation of over 100 East Bloc diplomatic personnel found on the island—Soviet, East German, Bulgarian and Libyan. Arrangements were made for the Cubans until they could be returned to Havana, and for PRA troops to be screened and released (except for senior officers). US intelligence officers began examination of the tons of documents captured, including secret treaties between the NJM and other Communist governments, lists of aid supplied, and detailed accounts of Soviet intelligence activities in the western hemisphere. At the Calivigny Camp US troops found a complete training centre for South American terrorists, complete with classrooms, weapons range and field training sites. Also

USAF C-141 *Starlifter* **of 63rd MAW, normally based at Norton AFB, California rolls to a stop in front of 82nd Airborne personnel whom it will carry back to the United States. (USAF)**

captured were the centre's personnel files, with names, biographies and photographs of the graduating classes. All of these would be circulated among the police of interested countries. Most of the 82nd troops were withdrawn in November, returning to Ft Bragg and a tumultuous reception from families and local civilians. If anything, the Marines had an even more appreciative group awaiting them in Lebanon—the personnel of 24th MAU whom they were relieving!

Costs and Lessons

The Grenada operation cost the lives of 18 American servicemen—11 soldiers, three Marines and four Navy SEALs. A nineteenth soldier later died of his wounds. In all, 116 US personnel were wounded on the island. Material losses are harder to establish, but officially include nine or ten helicopters lost or damaged. Cuban casualties numbered 25 dead and 59 wounded. No official attempt was made to separate Grenadian casualties into PRA and civilian totals; the combined figure was 45 dead and 350 wounded. All US combat forces were withdrawn by mid-December. One Army MP Company now remains to support the police.

Politically, 'Urgent Fury' represented an important change in American policy in the Caribbean. After the operation was over, there were several attempts to either ridicule its motives ('I believe our government has a responsibility to go to the aid of its citizens if their right to life and liberty is threatened,' said President Reagan on 27 October; 'the

USMC LVPT-7 command vehicle of the 2nd Amphibious Assault Company at LZ 'RACETRACK', Queen's Park Race Course, after the relief of the SEAL team at Government House. This vehicle has a crew of 13 and is equipped with additional radios, a generator and an air filtration system. (USMC)

nightmare of our hostages in Iran must never be repeated'); or to downplay its significance. Domestically, the first attempt was doomed when the rescued medical students returned to the United States. Seeing them kiss the ground as they disembarked from Air Force transports, the average American knew the same pride in his armed forces that Britons felt on the recovery of the Falklands. Internationally, the effusive welcome the Grenadian people gave to the US and Caribbean forces served much the same purpose.

The loss of Grenada was a severe blow to Cuban prestige worldwide and, more directly, to its plans in the region. Within days, several Caribbean countries had broken ties with Havana and expelled Cuban personnel. The exposure of the secret agreements with East Bloc countries fully revealed the subversive process in action. As many Grenadians expressed it, US intervention had really come 'just in time'. When President Reagan chose to call the operation 'a rescue mission', the Grenadians eagerly adopted the term, and there was no doubt in their minds as to what they had been rescued from. Regrettably, a year later, the island has still not recovered politically from its experience of the NJM.

Militarily, the chief significance of 'Urgent Fury'

was to demonstrate the readiness, capability and professionalism of the US armed forces. The entire operation was planned and carried out in less than a week. While operating under stringent rules of engagement, American personnel accomplished their missions with prudence and valour. 'I can't say enough in praise of our military,' President Reagan said; 'Army Rangers and paratroops, Navy, Marine and Air Force personnel, those who planned a brilliant campaign and those who carried it out.' In war, as in all human endeavours, it is not possible to foresee every possibility; yet, when plans went awry, in every case the training and flexibility of US forces overcame the obstacle. The military skills of every participant were tested and found sound. Hopefully, the Grenada operation will serve a similar purpose to the Falklands war, as a symbol of military professionalism and a national resolve to keep faith with its citizens in peril.

The 4th Platoon, 2nd Amphibious Assault Co. regroups at LZ 'RACETRACK' on Wednesday 26 October. Generally known as the 'amtrack', the LVPT-7 is the standard USMC personnel carrier. It can carry 25 passengers as well as a crew of three, and is armed with a .50cal. turret-mounted machine gun. A UH-46D of HMM-261, workhorse of the campaign, waits behind it. (USMC)

Notes on Helicopter Losses

After some research, the authors believe the following were lost or irreparably damaged during the operation.

Date	Army	Marine Corps
25 Oct.	1 Hughes 500HD *Defender*, 1 UH-60 *Blackhawk*	2 AH-1T *SeaCobras*
26 Oct.		1 UH-46D *Sea Knight*
27 Oct.	2 UH-60 *Blackhawks* (constructive total loss)	
	1 UH-60 *Blackhawk* (major damage)	
	1 OH-58 *Kiowa* (major damage)	
	3 UH-60 *Blackhawks* (minor damage)	
Total	4 aircraft lost 2 aircraft, major damage	3 aircraft lost
Final Total	9 aircraft lost or badly damaged; 3 aircraft, minor damage	

Some of the building materials for the unfinished Point Salines terminal facility have here been pressed into use as a revetment for a Marine UH-46D. Behind, a C-141 *Starlifter* heads for home with Army Rangers. (USMC)

Notes on Unit Designations

Due to the current, somewhat cumbersome US Army designations of its units, the authors have chosen to use an earlier, shorter version. For accuracy, however, please note that the proper designation of, for example, the 2/325th Airborne Infantry is: 2d BN(ABN) 325th INF.

The Plates

A1: Delta Force, Special Operations Command
In the wake of the Iran hostage crisis, the United States decided to acquire a counter-terrorist capability in the early 1980s. A special Joint Services Task Force was organised to fill this rôle. Details are sparse: although it is known to be part of the Army's Special Operations Command, no details of the unit's existence, composition or activities have ever been released. Even its precise designation is classified. The unit is known to have operated under several codenames, and is com-monly referred to as 'Delta Force' by the Press. A second theory suggests that no such permanent unit actually exists, and that the codenames refer instead to *ad hoc* task forces out of the 1st Special Forces at Ft Bragg. Whichever is correct, personnel of this unit were employed on Grenada.

There was supposedly wide variation in weapons and personal equipment. This trooper wears the plain OD (Olive Drab) jungle fatigues without insignia (both plain and slanted pocket types were worn) with standard Jungle Boots. Load-bearing equipment includes a STABO Extraction Harness and LC-2 Pistol Belt. Attached to the harness is a Gerber Mk.II knife and an Air Force strobe light. Worn on the belt itself are two standard canteens and a third, Two-Quart Canteen Carrier, em-ployed as a pack. It contains a flare projector, certain components of an MRE Ration (Meal, Ready to Eat), half of a two-part survival kit, etc. A standard Army flashlight completes the soldier's equipment. His weapon is the folding-stock Uzi 9 mm SMG with improved Sionics sound sup-pressor. Sixteen 32-round magazines for the weapon are carried in a magazine case on the belt. Extra equipment of unknown nature was carried in various kitbags.

A2: US Army Ranger, 2/75th Ranger Battalion

The origin of the American Rangers dates back to the French and Indian Wars of the 18th century. The designation was resurrected during World War II for the six Ranger battalions formed for Commando-type missions on the British model. Dissolved after the war, the Rangers were briefly re-formed as independent companies for Korea. After that war, the units were again broken up; henceforward the title 'Ranger' applied only to graduates of the Army's Ranger School at Ft Benning, Georgia. The school taught mountaineering and fieldcraft in a physically punishing environment, and individual graduates received a coveted black and yellow shoulder title for their uniforms. During the Vietnam War the Long Range Reconnaissance units formed by individual commands in Vietnam were all collectively re-designated as Ranger Companies in the 75th Infantry Regiment. At that time, they were also given the insignia and battle honours of the famous World War II 'Merrill's Marauders'. Finally, in the mid-1970s, two permanent Ranger battalions were formed: 1/75th at Ft Stewart, Georgia and 2/75th at Ft Lewis, Washington.

Both units jumped at Point Salines, using T-10 parachutes rather than the newer MC-1. Because of the low altitude from which they jumped, the 2/75th were ordered to discard their reserve parachutes. Current procedures call for rucksacks to be carried upside-down beneath the reserve

Marine riflemen board a CH-46 aboard the LPH *Guam* **for the short hop to Grenada. (USMC)**

'chute. Apparently, due to the speed with which they 'packed' in the crowded C-130s, many men elected to jump with their equipment rigged as shown. Weapons, ammunition and water were all that was carried; even so, most men carried well over 100 lbs of equipment when they jumped.

A3: Aircrewman, 16th Special Ops. Sqn., USAF

This AC-130 Spectre crewman wears standard CWU-27 flight suit, steel-toed flying boots and GR-FRP-1 flying gloves. The SRU-21 survival vest has an attached leather holster for an S&W Model 10 revolver. In the pockets of the vest are a URC-68 Survival Radio, flares, strobe light, compass, etc. Over this is worn the LPU-10 Life Preserver (under-arm type) and, finally, the parachute harness which takes a 28-ft-canopy chest-type Emergency Reserve. A pilots' survival knife is secured to the chest strap of the harness. The helmet is the HGU-26P with M87 dynamic microphone for communication with other crew members: as per current Tactical Air Command practice, it is covered in Woodland pattern camouflage material.

B1: US Army Ranger, 2/75th Ranger Battalion

In common with other Rangers, this man wears Jungle Boots, Vietnam-era hot-weather fatigues, and the all-nylon web gear designated the ALICE System (for All-purpose, Lightweight, Individual Combat Equipment). Individual components are designated in the LC (Lightweight Combat) series. The standard set comprises Belt Suspenders, LC-2 Pistol Belt (with quick-release buckle improved over the LC-1 type), Field Dressing Pouch, two Ammunition Pouches and two plastic canteens in carriers. His weapon is the M203 rifle/grenade launcher, which combines a pump-action 40 mm grenade launcher with the standard M-16 rifle. Its rounds are carried in a special Grenadier's Vest; made of nylon mesh and cotton duck, it holds 24 rounds. In addition to M-67 grenades carried on ammo pouches, a Snap Ring, used in rappelling from helicopters, is also attached. Instead of the PASGT armour vest the black Hardcore Second Chance type is worn; in general, on Grenada, it was used only by vehicle drivers who had remained aboard the C-130s and came in afterwards. The plain OD M1951 Patrol Cap, with its distinctive 'crush', is now unique to the Rangers: the rest of the

Paratroops move inland from Point Salines, every man with a LAW anti-tank weapon strapped to his rucksack. The grenadier at right wears the nylon ammunition vest for his M203 weapon. Twenty rounds of 40 mm grenades (high explosive and multiple projectile) go in the lower pockets, four white star cluster or parachute signal cartridges in the upper. (US Army)

Army uses the same cap but in Woodland camouflage. As Army élite troops, Rangers are authorised a black beret with Service Dress, but, unlike the Paratroops and Special Forces, they never take their berets into the field.

B2: US Army Ranger, 2/75th Ranger Battalion

In addition to his normal ALICE equipment, this 2/75th rifleman wears the unique ammunition vest issued only to this battalion. Developed by a private contractor, who arranged a gratuitous issue to the unit, it was designed to carry various types of magazines and grenades. Apparently several different patterns were provided for testing. In the field, the metal pin-on rank insignia normally worn on the collar (see Plate B1) are often omitted. Four M-59 Fragmentation grenades are carried attached to ammo pouches, and an M-7 Bayonet in Scabbard M8A1 is attached to the LC-2 Pistol Belt.

B3: US Army Ranger, 1/75th Ranger Battalion

The little-known 90 mm M67 Recoilless Rifle was developed in the early 1960s as a company anti-tank weapon. In most of the Army it has since been replaced by guided missiles; however, because of its light weight, it remains in use with the Ranger battalions. Their gunners had an excellent chance to demonstrate its effectiveness at Point Salines! Remaining A/T rounds and the ever-present Light Anti-tank Weapon (LAW) are carried in this man's ALICE pack. His personal weapon is a CAR-15, a shortened version of the M-16 rifle. (The current CAR-15 differs slightly from the Vietnam version, in, for example, using the barrel and flash suppressor of the standard rifle.) The back of the gunner's Patrol Cap also shows the luminous 'catseyes' used on all combat headgear for stationkeeping on night patrol. The fingerless gloves, taken from a photograph, seem to be cut down from the standard dress gloves. Also note the 1/75th scroll displayed on the left arm; it differs slightly from that worn by the 2nd Bn., as shown on other figures in this Plate.

C1: US Marine Machine Gunner, 2/8th Marines, 22nd MAU

The Marines taking part in 'Urgent Fury' were dressed in the new camouflage Battledress Uniform, usually referred to as 'BDUs'. This was adopted by the Army and Marine Corps in 1981 to replace all other field clothing in use. Made of a 50/50 nylon-cotton fabric for greater burn protection, the uniform was the subject of criticism even before Grenada. Some odd features of its styling, as well as the fabric itself, made it hot and uncomfortable in warm climates. A lighter weight Tropical BDU uniform has since been developed. With it is worn standard ALICE gear and the new PASGT (Personal Armor System, Ground Troops) body armour. Made of Kevlar, the vest provides protection against both bullets and shrapnel; older US body armour protects against shrapnel alone.[1] Metal pin-on rank insignia is displayed on the flap. As a machine gunner, this man is also issued a .45 pistol and Kabar knife. The pistol's spare magazine pouch is also attached to the vest, a common practice. In anticipation of forthcoming MNF duties in Lebanon, American flag patches were sewn on the left sleeve; they were felt appropriate for Grenada, and were left in place.

C2: US Navy SEAL, SEAL Team Four

The SEALs, the US Navy's special forces, had their origin in the early 1960s. (The name refers to their Sea, Air, Land, capabilities.) Basically, they are UDT personnel ('frogmen') who receive additional training in unconventional warfare. The SEALs achieved a high reputation in Vietnam. Two units were employed in Grenada, Teams Four and Six. (A SEAL Team is a platoon-size unit.) Their performance was mixed; they accomplished some, but not all of their assignments, and suffered a number of casualties. It should be recalled, however, that they were assigned very difficult missions to begin with. This man's uniform is the older 100 per cent cotton Woodland type, with hat. Supplementing his LC-2 web gear is an Air Force Pilot's SRV-21P survival vest, modified to carry magazine pockets and the holster for a S&W Model 39 pistol. A variety of individual weapons were carried. This man's Ingram M-10, equipped with

sound suppressor, is typical; others include the World War II M-3 'Grease Gun' and the Heckler & Koch MP5, also silenced. A Gerber Mk. II knife and a strobe light are worn on the belt.

C3: US Marine Rifleman, 2/8th Marines, 22nd MAU

Stripped to his olive-green T-shirt (now used only by the Marine Corps), this Marine shows a rear view of the LC-2 webbing. The rectangular pouch at the rear of the belt is the Jungle First Aid kit; while part of the ALICE system, it is used only by the Marine Corps. Not all Marines were issued Jungle Boots, and this man has the ordinary DMS (Direct Moulded Sole) type.

An 82nd Airborne major examines some of the 1,600-odd AKMs captured on Grenada. The huge number of weapons captured, far more than the tiny PRA could use, clearly indicates that Grenada was intended to be a major staging area for guerrilla insertions into South America. Venezuela, for example, rich in oil and minerals, is less than 100 miles away. (US Army)

[1]For a full account of body armour development and current practice, see MAA 157 *Flak Jackets: 20th Century Military Body Armour.*

President and Mrs Reagan with Sgt. Stephen Trujillo, 2/75th Rangers. Sgt. Trujillo, a medic, was awarded the Silver Star for his rescue of wounded under fire at the Calivigny Camp on 27 October. In an unusual gesture, he was presented to a Joint Session of Congress by the President, to represent the men who fought in Grenada. For the ceremony, the sergeant wears his Winter Service uniform with black Ranger beret and 2/75th 'flash'. (White House)

D1: US Army Grenadier, 2/325th Infantry (Airborne), 82nd Airborne Division

The 82nd Airborne Division was the first unit to receive the new Kevlar helmet, developed as part of the PASGT System. Because of its Germanic shape it was immediately dubbed the 'Fritz' by the Army. Any problem with its appearance was quickly forgotten on Grenada; the new helmet was credited with saving the lives of at least two paratroopers. The 82nd received a special Paratroop model of the 'Fritz', with a different internal suspension from the model issued to ground troops. The rest of this grenadier's equipment is the standard ALICE nylon web gear, with 40 mm grenade rounds carried in Vietnam-era plastic slip-on carriers. (The standard method of carrying these rounds is the nylon vest shown in Plate B, but the 325th also used the type shown here.) Extra rifle ammunition is carried in cotton bandoliers secured across the body. A LAW anti-tank rocket is secured to the

soldier's pack. The carrier for the protective mask at the man's waist is worn secured for jumping with a strip of tape; after arrival on the island, many paratroops did not bother to remove the tape. BDU sleeves are rolled up in the approved Army fashion, which leaves the camouflage pattern outermost.

D2: US Army Dragon A/T Gunner, 2/505th Infantry (Airborne), 82nd Airborne Division

The wire-guided M47 Dragon missile is the Army's medium-range anti-tank weapon. Launcher, base and sights fold neatly into this configuration for carrying. Seen from this angle, the gunner also presents a good view of the ALICE Medium Pack. Shown attached to its right side is the standard two-quart canteen. Helmet camouflage policy varies in the 82nd by battalion: some units use only the Woodland cover while others, 2/505th among them, specify additional strips of burlap to help break up the helmet's outline. Similarly, strips of tape are used to camouflage the stock and foregrip of the rifle. This soldier has also carried out a standard, although unauthorised modification to his M-16, improvising an assault sling from the standard issue. An unsatisfactory and potentially dangerous practice (rigged in this fashion, the sling can easily jam the bolt retraction handle), this was nevertheless common on Grenada. Other troops improvised assault slings from various straps and ropes, a slightly better method. Once on the island, many soldiers found the Army method of folding up BDU sleeves too time-consuming, and simply rolled them up in a normal fashion.

D3: US Army Sniper, 1/508th Infantry (Airborne), 82nd Airborne Division

In the American Army the maroon beret was first introduced (unofficially) for Airborne troops in the mid-1970s. Permission for its wear was withdrawn in 1979, but reinstated a year later. As with other units authorised a beret (Special Forces and Rangers), it is worn with a shield-shaped 'flash' in the unit colours. Centred on the flash officers wear metal rank insignia, and enlisted men the distinctive metal unit crest. Not all 82nd troops wore BDUs in Grenada; some still had the older cotton Woodland uniform. The standard Army sniper weapon is the 7.62 mm M-21 rifle, used with the Redfield Accutrack riflescope offering a

Awaiting orders at Point Salines, soldiers of the Barbados and Dominican or St Vincent contingents adjust kit. The Barbadians wear green berets and British DPM camouflage fatigues; the other troops, dark blue berets and OD fatigues.

See also Plate G. Caribbean forces were assigned duties commensurate with their training: these soldiers carried out joint patrols with US troops, while police personnel guarded prisoners.

Briefing for St Vincent PKF personnel is given by an 82nd officer. The St Vincent contingent consisted of constabulary-type police, dressed in Jamaican-made uniforms with US Jungle Boots and steel helmets and commercial pattern (?) body armour. A blue beret is also worn. (US Army)

variable capacity of 3 to 9 power. This man also carries a pair of M-19 general field use binoculars.

E1: Private First Class, Grenada People's Revolutionary Army

This soldier wears the standard PRA combat uniform, provided by Cuba and slightly modified by the wearer: i.e. addition of shoulder straps, shortening of sleeves, etc. The steel helmet is of Soviet manufacture, but considerably different from the older Soviet model: it appears to combine design features from the East German *Helm 56* and the Soviet model. It is uncertain whether this is an export model (the same helmet has been supplied to certain African countries under Soviet influence) or a new Soviet Army model which will replace the style now in service. Standard Soviet/Cuban load-bearing gear is worn with the addition of the folding entrenching-tool of East German manufacture, virtually identical to the late World War II German Army model. The rucksack worn is standard issue in the Soviet Army and remains basically unchanged since World War I. Boots are of Cuban manufacture. The weapon is the RPG-7 of Soviet manufacture.

E2: PRA Armour Crewman

The Cuban-supplied tanker's coveralls are made of 100 per cent cotton and incorporate a drop seat in the rear—a very useful feature. They are worn with the Soviet tank helmet and Cuban combat boots. The Czech Model 25 sub-machine gun, large

numbers of which were captured on the island, is also Cuban-supplied.

E3: Cuban construction worker

The Cuban workers fighting against the Americans did so in a variety of civilian work, sports and casual clothing. Minimal accoutrements are worn; here, a leather equipment belt and an AKM magazine pouch holding three clips. The straw hat is also a very typical Cuban item.

F1: Cuban Army Advisor to PRA

This *teniente* (lieutenant) of the *Fuerzas Armadas Revolucionarias* (FAR = Revolutionary Armed Forces) wears the standard Cuban Army combat uniform. The 'Castro hat' is identical to the US M1951 Field Cap from which it was derived. Similarly, the fatigue/combat shirt is virtually identical to a US Army fatigue shirt of the 1950s. The combat trousers show some attempt at originality in the addition of single snap-closure cargo pockets; these, however, are so poorly designed as to be totally useless. The load-bearing equipment (suspenders, pistol belt, canteen, magazine pouch) are of standard Soviet pattern and manufacture. The only notable difference is the polished steel belt buckle, which bears the old heraldic shield of the Cuban Republic (retained by the Communist government) stamped upon it in high relief. The magazine pouch holds three 30-round magazines for the AKM, as well as a double-spout oiler and a cleaning/spare-parts kit. All the equipment illustrated appears to be standard Soviet export—identical materiel is supplied to Afghanistan and African nations under Soviet influence. Around the neck (underneath the ubiquitous religious medals) is worn a black plastic marching compass, manufactured by the old German firm of Freiberger Präzisionsmechanik, now located in the Eastern Zone, as indicated by the 'NVA' stamp on the crystal (NVA = *Nationale Volksarmee*).

F2: Captain, Soviet Spetsnaz Advisor

The *Spetsnaz* (*Spetsialnoye Naznachenye* = Special Purpose), sometimes referred to as Soviet Special Forces, are a little-known branch of Soviet Army intelligence, equivalent to the US Special Forces or the British SAS. Their wartime mission consists of long-range reconnaissance and raider-type operations, but in peacetime they are also available for various types of covert activity. A number were present on Grenada, apparently serving as instructors. Two became casualties fighting against American forces; the remainder were detained with the Soviet diplomatic staff on the island. Awaiting repatriation via Mexico, they suffered a final indignity at the airport: American soldiers searched their baggage and relieved them of their weapons before allowing them to depart! While serving on Grenada the *Spetsnaz* wore the Soviet tropical uniform of hat, jacket and trousers, all of thick, coarsely woven cotton, and Soviet tropical boots of thin, poor-quality leather. Rank insignia is worn in the form of 'subdued' field shoulder boards. The officer holds the Soviet PM2 10-Cap blasting machine.

F3: PRM Militiawoman, Rapid Mobilisation Company
The Grenadian People's Revolutionary Militia was intended by the NJM to fulfil several rôles, including involving the masses in political action and providing local security against sabotage and subversion. The PRM was also to provide a 5,000-member reserve for the armed forces. Like other NJM projects, it was less than a total success. Due to equipment shortages and administrative failings, few PRM even received uniforms or weapons training. The best militia units were the Rapid Mobilisation Companies, one of which was provided for each PRA Defence Region. Despite their generally pro-Bishop leaning, many militiamen fought enthusiastically against the invasion on the first day. As in many Third World revolutionary states, women were conspicuously encouraged to bear arms. This woman PRM wears a Cuban pack and web gear over standard PRA fatigues. Ammunition for her Czech Model 52 rifle is carried in Czech-supplied belt pouches. Her uniform and equipment were a rarity in the militia; most members had only civilian clothes.

G1: Private, Barbados Contingent, Caribbean Peace-keeping Force
Barbados contributed both military forces and police to the Grenada operation. Included were two troops of Support Squadron, Barbados Defence Force (about 60 men) and 50 members of the Royal Barbados Police. The Chief of Staff of the BDF, Brig. Rudyard Lewis, commanded the Peacekeep-

An M102 105 mm battery in action at Point Salines. Note construction material used for emplacements. (US Army)

ing Forces (PKF) sent to Grenada, being responsible for their reception, administration and support while on Barbados. In addition, the Barbados government made available Grantley Adams International Airport to support the operation. The BDF is outfitted with a mixture of British and American items, including British tropical DPM uniforms and US Jungle Boots. The American steel helmet is worn in the British fashion with either DPM cover, or netting, or both, as preferred. The complete '58 Pattern web gear is worn; and British weapons, such as the SLR and the L4A2 LMG (shown here) are used. The blue armband was issued to all Caribbean Forces as identification during the operation. Note the green beret, with badge moved inside for combat operations.

G2: Private, Jamaican Contingent, Caribbean Peace-keeping Force

Of the six Caribbean nations sending forces to Grenada (Dominica, St Lucia, St Vincent, Antigua, Barbados and Jamaica), Jamaica contributed the largest number of troops—152 officers and men from 'B' Co., 2nd Bn., Jamaica Regiment, JDF. Col. K. Barnes of the JDF served as ground commander of the PKF in Grenada. The JDF is also equipped with British weapons and '58 web gear, but their uniforms are manufactured locally. Other Caribbean forces purchased these uniforms for their own forces; the JDF may be distinguished by British helmets, and, sometimes, British boots and puttees. The rifle green berets bear a crowned star badge in brass, with a silver and black central device showing a map of the island in a scroll.

G3: Constable, Royal Barbados Police, Caribbean Peacekeeping Force

Of six Caribbean countries participating in 'Urgent Fury', four could contribute only police. Jamaica sent only soldiers, and Barbados, as mentioned, both soldiers and police. (A seventh country, St Kitts-Nevis, later sent a small police contingent.) The individual police units were of widely varied military value. The Dominica and St Vincent contingents, for example, dressed in combat uniforms and had military training and weaponry. Other nations had police more in the British tradition. They had only their brightly coloured dress uniforms, and no weapons training at all. The Royal Barbados Police were somewhere in the middle. They had firearms training, but no weapons. The US provided M-16s and basic ALICE gear of belt, suspenders and ammo pouches. This man, taken from a photo, has his own '58 web gear (from RBP reserve stocks), but has armed himself with a Soviet assault rifle. His uniform is basically similar to other contingents. The red trouser stripe identifies him as a member of the RBP. The Antiguan Police had white cap bands and trouser stripes; St Lucia's, plain blue caps.

G4: Military Policewoman, 16th MP Brigade, US XVIII Airborne Corps

A variety of Army support units served on Grenada, most provided by the 82nd Airborne Division or its parent XVIII Airborne Corps. (Also included, however, were medical personnel from Ft Bragg, and transportation units from Ft Eustis and Ft

Grenadian civilians anxiously watch Marine patrol on the second day of the invasion. Note the Marines' leather combat boots and distinguishing Jungle First Aid Pouch. (USMC)

Storey, Virginia.) In general, airborne units wore the BDU uniform, and non-airborne personnel, brand new OD jungle fatigues without any insignia. Headgear for everyone was either the M1 Steel Helmet (with Woodland cover) or the camouflage version of the M1951 Patrol Cap. Four companies of Military Police were eventually sent to Grenada, the 82nd's MP Company and the 21st, 65th and 108th MP Companies from the XVIII Corps' 16th MP Brigade. The Brigade headquarters and the headquarters of the 503rd MP Battalion also deployed. The 108th included four women, in the first real test of a controversial policy.

Starting in the mid-1970s, all the US Armed Forces began to offer expanded career opportunities for women, and, at present, they are excluded from only a handful of military specialties. A complicated formula determines to what extent they may be exposed to combat, and there was some confusion on Grenada. When their unit arrived on 29 October, the four women were mistakenly returned to Ft Bragg. This action, although well-intentioned, was determined to be inconsistent with current policy, and the women rejoined their company to become the first of 116 women to serve on Grenada. They guarded newsmen, flew helicopters and loaded cargo planes, with only an occasional surprised glance from male counterparts. The Army makes minimal concessions to female personnel; field uniforms and equipment are the same as for males. Woman MPs, however, carry a .38 revolver as a personal weapon rather than a .45. In the field, an M-16 is the basic weapon of both. As airborne troops, all XVIII Corps personnel are authorised the red beret, worn here with the MP Brigade's flash and Corps troops' distinctive insignia. Only 82nd MP Co. personnel had the 'Fritz' helmet; everyone else wore the M1C type.

H1: US Navy A-7 Corsair Pilot, VA-15, USS Independence

This pilot is wearing the equipment common to all high-performance fighter/attack aircraft. The flight suit is the CWU-27 model with a flap added to the pen/pencil holder to prevent Foreign Object Damage to engine. The boots are the steel-toed flyers' type; gloves are the GR-FRP-1, of fire-resistant Nomex and leather. Over the thighs and abdomen is worn the Mk.2 Gravity Suit for anti-

Marines of F Co., 2/8th Marine Regt. make a house-to-house search for PRA officials in Georgetown on Friday 28 October. This angle affords a good view of the PASGT body armour from the rear. (USMC)

blackout protection; over this, the MA-2 Torso Harness which doubles as restraint to the ejection seat and parachute harness as well. Over everything is worn the SV-2A Survival Vest and LPA-1a Life Preserver, which provides 35 lbs of buoyancy around the waist and neck. The survival vest contains everything a pilot will require if shot down in unfriendly territory: survival knife, RT-90 Radio, 24-hour SRU-31 Survival Kit, strobe light, pen flare projector and, depending on the nature of the mission, a revolver. The helmet is the APH-6C Dual-visor for multi-rôle use, painted in VA-15's blue and gold squadron colours. The oxygen mask is the A-13A Pressure Breathing Mask, made of silicone for greater comfort.

H2: US Marine Helicopter Pilot, HMM-261 (Reinforced)

This AH-1T *Cobra* pilot, attached from HML-167, wears the CWU-27 flight suit and boots and gloves for flying personnel. Personal survival gear is identical to a fixed wing pilot's, with the exception of the SV-2A Vest, which has an adjustable V-Ring added to the top for helicopter extraction. This helmet is the SPH-3B for rotary wing personnel, standard issue since 1966. It features two visors (neutral grey and clear) and superior comfort and sound attenuation. At almost 4 lbs it is, however, heavy. In common with other Marines, an American flag patch is displayed on the left sleeve.

H3: US Army Helicopter Pilot, 82nd Combat Aviation Battalion, 82nd Airborne Division

This UH-60 *Blackhawk* pilot is wearing the standard flying equipment issued to all Army aircrew, including the CWU-27 Flight Suit, GR-FRP-1 gloves and the steel-toed boots used in all flying operations. The helmet worn is the SPH-4C, originally introduced in the late 1960s for both fixed and rotary-wing aircrew. Unlike its Navy counterpart, the SPH-3B, it features only a single visor, but this can be interchanged as the mission dictates.

Both Army and Navy helmets feature improved sound attenuation, which gives them their bulged-ear appearance. Current Army practice is to leave the helmet in its original Olive Drab factory finish. This particular crewman is also wearing the aircrew 'Chickenplate' Armor Vest, originally introduced in Vietnam. Intended to stop high velocity projectiles, it has been known to stop even 12.7 mm rounds on occasion! The SRU-27 Survival Vest can be worn over the armour, if required.

Notes sur les planches en couleur

A1 La tenue et l'équipement varient beaucoup à l'intérieur de cette unité spéciale. L'équipement de cet homme comprend le harnais *STABO* pour enlèvement par hélicoptère. **A2** Sautant à basse altitude, cette unité se débarrassa de ses sacs de parachutage de réserve, qui constituaient un poids supplémentaire inutile. 45 kg d'armes, de munitions et d'eau sont transportés. **A3** Tenue de vol standard et 'gilet de survie', harnais de parachute et veste de survie. Le gilet permet de transporter une radio, des fusées, des rations, un revolver, etc.

B1 Le calot vert simple n'est maintenant porté que par les Rangers. Le gilet de munitions contient 24 grenades pour le lance-grenades 40 mm/fusil combiné M203. Le béret noir des Rangers n'est pas porté sur le terrain. **B2** Par contraste, ce gilet de munitions appartient exclusivement à cette unité—c'est un modèle commercial distribué gratuitement par le fabricant, avec des poches pour divers types de chargeurs et de grenades. **B3** Notez les triangles lumineux fixés à l'arrière du calot, les munitions pour le fusil sans recul M67 et la roquette *LAW*, portées dans le sac; et le pistolet automatique CAR-15.

C1 Uniforme de corvée de camouflage 'terrain boisé'—les 'BDU' firent leur apparition en 1981. Il porte l'équipement en toile de sangles ALICE, le blindage *PASGT* ainsi que l'insigne de drapeau américain déjà porté sur la manche gauche par cette unité, qui se rendait au Liban. **C2** En plus de l'équipement en toile de sangles LC-2 (*ALICE*), il porte un gilet de survie SRU-21P de l'armée de l'air, modifié pour le combat; notez le pistolet automatique silencieux Ingram. **C3** Vue arrière de l'équipement en toile de sangles LC-2; sac de premiers secours de jungle et tee-shirt vert; ces deux articles sont maintenant exclusifs aux Marines.

D1 Le casque *Kevlar*, qui s'est révélé très efficace, fut porté pour la première fois durant cette campagne; les parachutistes de la 82e division avaient un modèle à la courroie spéciale. **D2** Notez le missile anti-char Dragon plié pour le transport; le sac *ALICE Medium Pack* sur le dos; et une 'bandoulière d'assaut' improvisée pour le fusil. **D3** Le béret de parachutiste rouge foncé fut finalement autorisé en 1980, après une période de confusion. Il porte le fusil M-21 de tireur d'élite.

E1 Uniforme cubain légèrement modifié; équipement soviétique standard, avec outil de tranchée de l'Allemagne de l'est; lance-roquettes *RPG-7*; et un casque intéressant de fabrication soviétique qui diffère du modèle soviétique standard. **E2** L'équipage des *BTR-60* de Grenade portait cette tenue communiste standard et des pistolets automatiques M25 tchèques. **E3** Tenue de civil, avec équipement minimal.

F1 Uniforme cubain standard (notez la boucle de la ceinture) et équipement soviétique, avec fusil d'assaut *AKM*. **F2** Plusieurs des ces officiers des Forces spéciales se trouvaient à Grenade; deux étaient blessés dans les combats contre les forces américaines, le reste fut déporté. Tenue d'été de l'armée soviétique standard, avec épaulettes de rang de modèle feld. **F3** Femme appartenant aux gardes nationaux, exceptionnellement bien équipée, des compagnies d'élite de mobilisation rapide, avec équipement cubain et fusil M52 tchèque.

G1 Les troupes de Barbades portent des tenues de camouflage *DPM* britanniques; l'insigne sur le béret vert a été déplacé pour être porté à l'intérieur de la coiffe, le casque est américain, l'équipement en toile de sangles et les armes sont britanniques—ici, la mitraillette légère *L4A2*. **G2** Armes et équipement en toile de sangles britanniques, uniformes verts de confection locale, casques et bérets vert foncé distinguent les troupes de la Jamaïque. Tous les contingents portent le brassard bleu pour être rapidement identifiés. **G3** Les agents de police aux uniformes de couleur n'étaient utilisés que pour garder les prisonniers. **G4** Environ 116 femmes servirent avec les forces américaines à Grenade; de nos jours, seules certaines missions de combat sont déniées aux femmes.

H1 Equipement de vol standard complet des équipages des avions à réaction rapides américains. Le casque bleu et or représente une coutume d'escadron du personnel des VA-15. **H2** Essentiellement la même tenue, mais les pilotes d'hélicoptères n'ont pas d'harnais de parachutiste ou de 'G-Suits' et portent un casque de vol différent. **H3** Les pilotes de l'armée portent ce casque à visière unique. Notez le blindage de corps '*chickenplate*', qui a arrêté des balles de 12,7 mm!

Farbtafeln

A1 Diese Spezialeinheit verfügt über viele verschiedene Uniform- und Zubehörvariationen. Dieser Mann hat ein *STABO*-Gurtwerk für Sprünge aus dem Hubschrauber. **A2** Wegen der Sprünge aus geringer Höhe warf diese Einheit ihre Reservefallschirme als Ballast ab. Die Soldaten trugen 100 Pfund an Waffen, Munition und Wasser. **A3** Üblicher Fliegeranzug sowie 'Lebensrettungsweste', Fallschirmgurtwerk und Schwimmweste. In der Weste trägt er das Radio, Leuchtkugeln, Kompass, Verpflegung, Revolver usw.

B1 Heute tragen nur die *Rangers* die einfache grüne Mütze. Die Munitionsweste enthält 24 Granaten für das M203 Kombinationsgewehr/40 mm Granatenwerfer. Die schwarze Feldmütze der *Rangers* wird nicht draussen im Einsatz getragen. **B2** Diese Munitionsweste gibt es nur bei dieser Einheit—sie ist ein Geschenk des Herstellers und hat Taschen für Magazine und Granaten. **B3** Beachten Sie die leuchtenden Dreiecke hinten an der Feldmütze, die Munition für das rückstossfreie M67-Gewehr und die *LAW*-Rakete, die der Soldat mit sich trägt, sowie die CAR-15-Maschinenpistole.

C1 Arbeitskleidung mit 'Wald'-Tarnung—'BDUs' tauchten 1981 auf. Er trägt *ALICE*-Ausrüstung, *PASGT*-Waffen und links am Arm die amerikanischen Flaggeninsignien, die diese Einheit auf ihrem Weg in den Libanon trug. **C2** Dieser Soldat trägt die LC-2 (*ALICE*) Ausrüstung sowie die SRU-21P Lebensrettungsweste der Marine, die für den Kampfeinsatz umgeändert wurde. Beachten Sie die Ingram-Maschinenpistole mit Schalldämpfer. **C3** Die LC-2-Ausrüstung von hinten sowie die Erste-Hilfe-Tasche für den Dschungel und grünes T-Shirt. Beides gehört zu den *Marines*.

D1 Ein *Kevlar*-Helm, der sich als sehr nützlich erwies. Er wurde in diesem Feldzug zum ersten Mal getragen. Die 82. Fallschirmjäger-Division verfügte über ein Modell mit speziellem *Dragon*-Panzerabwehrrakete sowie das *ALICE Medium Pack* auf dem Rücken und eine Schlinge am Gewehr. **D3** Die braune Feldmütze der Fallschirmjäger wurde nach einiger Verwirrung 1980 endlich zugelassen. Dieser Soldat trägt ein M-21-Scharfschützengewehr.

E1 Etwas abgeänderte kubanische Uniform, gewöhnliche sowietische Ausrüstung und Schützengrabenwerkzeug aus der DDR, *RPG-7*-Raketenwerfer sowie ein interessanter sowietischer Helm, der anders als die üblichen ist. **E2** Die Besatzung der *BTR-60* von Grenada trug diese normale kommunistische Kleidung sowie tschechische M25-Maschinenpistolen. **E3** Zivilkleidung mit wenig Zubehör.

F1 Übliche kubanische Uniform (beachten Sie die Gürtelschnalle) und sowietische Ausrüstung mit *AKM*-Angriffsgewehr. **F2** Mehrere Offiziere dieser Spezialeinheit kämpften an Grenada. Zwei verwundet im Kampf gegen die Amerikaner, und der Rest wurde deportiert. Übliche Sommeruniform der sowietischen Armee mit Feldpauletten, die den Rang angeben. **F3** Ungewöhnlich gut ausgerüstete Milizangehörige der Elitekompanien für 'Schnelle Mobilmachung' mit kubanischer Ausrüstung und tschechischem M52-Gewehr.

G1 Die Truppen von Barbados trugen britische *DPM*-Tarnuniform. Das Abzeichen an der grünen Feldmütze befindet sich hier innen. Der Helm ist amerikanisch, die Ausrüstung und Waffen sind britisch—hier trägt er ein leichtes *L4A2*-Maschinengewehr. **G2** Britische Waffen und Ausrüstung, einheimische, grüne Uniformen, britische Helme und dunkelgrün Feldmützen waren für Truppen aus Jamaika typisch. Alle Kontingente trugen blaue Armbinden, um sich gegenseitig leichter zu erkennen. **G3** Die Polizei in bunter Uniform bewachte die Gefangenen. **G4** Etwa 116 Frauen befanden sich unter den US-Truppen auf Grenada. Heutzutage werden Frauen nur bei sehr wenigen Kampfeinsätzen nicht zugelassen.

H1 Volle Fliegerausrüstung für die Besatzung der amerikanischen Fast Jets. Der blau-goldene Helm zeigt die VA-15-Schwadron an. **H2** Im Grossen und Ganzen dieselbe Uniform, aber Hubschrauberpiloten trugen weder Fallschirmgurtwerk noch 'G-Suits', und ausserdem haben sie einen anderen Helm. **H3** Die Piloten der Armee tragen diesen Helm mit einfachem Sichtschutz. Beachten Sie die '*Chickenplate*' Panzerweste, die angeblich 12,7 mm Kugeln abwehrt.